# MANAGING DEPRESSION

## An open greeting to life,love and genuine friendship

By Raymond Armstrong

# Table of content

# Presentation

On the off chance that you are feeling desolate as you are understanding this, you are in good company. The explanation
why I set up this book is on the grounds that I understand what it is like. Depression is a theme that is extremely near my heart since I have experienced the profundities of unfilled, futile sentiments ordinarily and I'm not new to that sort of feeling.

I have felt each grasping snapshot of it. The long, extended periods which appears as days, the forlorn evenings where I sob peacefully, dousing my cushion pungent with tears, the absence of want to confront the following day and the prospect of needing to end it
all!

It doesn't make any difference on the off chance that you have a sweetheart/beau, spouse or wife. Regardless how close you are with them, there are portions of you that they simply don't comprehend!.

The aggravation doesn't blur in the wake of trusting with your dearest companion, your gathering of mates, or even your instructor! No one appears to figure out you yet you believe that they should sympathize with your aggravation.

I sympathize with you, old buddy. I genuinely do. However, I have uplifting news for us all desolate hearts out there. I have made due through what's more, I have a method for tackling it on the off chance that not facilitate the aggravation in any event.

# Chapter1 :Isolated!

Everybody on the planet has felt this feeling some time. Particularly in
these times fast innovative development the sensation of depression is quickly
expanding. We, first and foremost, should explain what depression implies. Depression is a personal state. Here individuals experience a separation from individuals around them as well as a profound sensation of vacancy, which delivers their current organization around them unimportant. That individual could be in a major group or by him/herself, wedded or single, youthful or old. They fundamentally find it extremely difficult to interface with others and encounters liberation from significant connections. This isn't to mistaken for be distant from everyone else. Being separated from everyone else doesn't liken to being desolate in light of the fact that occasionally it is great for an individual to be separated from everyone else and on occasion it very well may be extremely reviving as the individual has the potential chance to invigorate, recover and rediscover part of our lives.

What are the normal side effects of being distant from everyone else, on the off chance that you are perusing this book? I wager you may be feeling one of these side effects.You think your concerns are extraordinary to the point that others don't have the foggiest idea.

Thus, you feel that others on the planet has companions and you don't

* You feel very reluctant in all that you do.

*You feel that when you accomplish something wrong, you get very humiliated

at the point when you are in a group, you feel suffocated by their voices.

*You feel separated with the group despite the fact that you are with them.Feeling modest and terrified of others encountering low confidence.

*Feeling irate, cautious and basic at everything regardless of whether it isn't aimed at you.

*Terrified of outsiders and decline to converse with participating in a good discussion

*Being persuaded something is off about you.

*Feeling restless and miserable accepting nobody knows how hopeless/confined you feel Losing your ability to confident' feel "undetectable" Declining to acknowledge change and don't have any desire to take a stab at anything new

*Feeling like essentially nothing else has any significance and considering self destruction.

# Chapter2:Swarmed At This Point Detached

At any point had that believing that your significant other or spouse doesn't grasp you? Your life partner or critical other is right alongside you yet it doesn't fill that hole. You might be encircled by many individuals, yet their organization 'suffocates' you more profound into depression!

Individuals have that impression since we are extraordinary and unique. You see:

There is nobody in the whole universe that will have similar character, thoughts, lifestyle and requirements like you. NONE! Not even twins! How might anybody satisfy all those requirements to cater each person?

There is a statement from the book of scriptures that says assuming that I attempt to eliminate the spot from my

neighbor's eye,i should initially eliminate the board from my OWN eye then I can see obviously before I endeavor to eliminate his bit.

**How does this apply?**

By understanding that others are not obliged to satisfy our requirements, we

some way or another figure out how to expect less from others and it facilitates the aggravation, since we quit hoping for something else from others! We figure out how to acknowledge them better and judge others less so it makes the initial step to relieving depression - giving others slack!

Recollect that we are the amount of the five individuals we invest the majority of our energy with.

Assuming you are blending in with a group that is negative and causes you to feel down all the time, it is nothing unexpected why you are desolate and negative. It is nothing unexpected that youngsters move out from their homes from negative guardians or stop connecting with specific gatherings of companions generally together. Try not to allow the toxic substance to deplete your energy.

# Chapter3:Close To Home Torments In A Cold World

How does the distress of depression appear to infiltrate the hearts of men and
ladies all through the world? Indeed, even hotshots who have been the symbol of
ages and appreciated by millions feel unfulfilled (for example Janis Joplin, Kurt
Cobain).
The sensation of depression is profoundly because of the disappointment of man in cherishing others. The side effects of forlornness charge the impacts of the aggravation to the degree that it powers the focal point of consideration more on ourselves and makes a self-distraction
that makes an obstruction to cherish others. At any point had a stomachache? Who are you considering at that point?
This delineates the point that we are just reasoning of ourselves.

It shows a frightfully torment filled world in which we live in. Moreover, the aggravation disappears like a stomachache. The alleged Midlife emergency is transforming more into a 'youthful grown-up' emergency now with self destruction rates stirring things up around town rooftop and most illnesses in this present reality intellectually actuated or restored in mental wards. The premise of trust between individuals is disintegrating and fewer and fewer individuals are opening dependent upon each other. By neglecting to open up to other people, the desolate side effects spring up as others won't open dependent upon you in the event that you don't open yourself to others first.

It is said that to be encircled by companions, be a companion to others first.

# Chapter4:Figuring Out How To Adore

How would I venture out to manage depression? By figuring out how to cherish. Above all we should inspect the conundrum to cherish. At the point when we are forlorn, we feel like we are in a deplorable jail. By its very nature of depression is very much like the stomach throb - the consideration fixates just on ourselves. So we attempt and fill this void by finding other people who will give us that very love we really want. Individuals frequently attempt to get things done for others to acquire their affection. They deal exchange favors with one another reasoning that they are cherishing individuals. We know that our depression
must be filled by the affection for other people and thusly we should feel adored by others. The conundrum of affection is this:
On the off chance that we try to make up for the shortfall of our own dejection in looking for affection from others, we will unavoidably find no relief except for just a more profound devastation.

At the end of the day, if we look for the love that we really want, we won't ever track down it. At the point when an individual situates his life towards the fulfillment of his own requirements, when he goes out to look for the love which he wants, he is essentially egotistical, no matter how forsaken he is. However long he centers around himself, his capacity to cherish will continuously stay hindered. What is the arrangement then?

On the off chance that an individual looks for not to get love, yet rather to give it without surprises, he will become adorable and he will definitely be cherished by others eventually. We should quit being worried about ourselves and start to be worried about others. Starting in light of the end - which centers the aftereffects of the demonstration of love others without worried about self-gain, is the initial step to acquiring love and facilitating the aggravation of depression. Everyone on earth has an ability to cherish.

We as a whole have a capacity to concentrate off ourselves to the requirements and worry of others. It is the degree that we will give, are we ready to get that measure of affection from others. Choosing to cherish others without any surprises resembles a gift (we don't anticipate anything consequently, not so much as a fulfilled inner self or eased culpability), not a bargain exchange. At the point when we ask others, "How have you helped me?" we have neglected to love. Regardless of whether toward the starting you are simply ready to adore close to nothing, you will be cherished close to nothing. That very love will enable you to develop and deliver more love and consequently get more prominent love from others. In any case, consistently recall that in making this self-gift or altruism, our psyches should continuously be centered away from ourselves or it wouldn't work.

# Chapter5:The Patterns Of Energy Attracting Similar Energy

As a man suspects, he is as well. At any point can't help thinking about why certain individuals get the amenable, aware, "Great Morning, Sir", and others get the, "Hello Bud" or "Hello, Macintosh" sort of treatment?

**Think briefly, presently.**

What is the contrast between Donald Trump and a transient other than two or three billion bucks furthermore, several high rises?

**The response: The soft inside your head.**

The manner in which individuals respond to you is because of the manner in which you ponder yourself. For what reason do
you think individuals pass judgment too quickly or a terrible kind by the garments he wears? I know it is unreasonable, however the manner in which an individual figures in his heart, he will show up or try and live out what he is thinking!.

The Pattern of energy attracting similar energy isn't a genuinely new thing; it is the status quo. It is obvious in

Murphy's Regulation - the things we most don't have any desire to happen to frequently happens to us, that is why a dropped buttered toast generally land on some unacceptable side! Indeed, even as a youngster in school, I have consistently trusted that when I saw sitting in class, and i didn't have the foggiest idea how to respond to an inquiry the educator posed, I generally murmured in my heart, "Don't pick me… Kindly, don't pick me" and the instructor generally did. It didn't make any difference where I was sitting, the educator had this clairvoyance power that realized I didn't have a clue about the reply or wasn't focusing. How does this apply to beating depression?

If you 'project' an atmosphere of lack of desirability, you will feel undesirable and your companions will reject you unwittingly. Quit behaving like a wet, undesirable pup who just got away from the pound. Share with yourself, "You track down me appealing, loveable and great organization."

It is valid we can't continuously persuade ourselves that we are adorable, appealing and individuals love being near us. However, since we have zero control over others' thought process, this type of attestation really tricks our mind into thinking WE ARE adorable and appealing.

# Chapter6:Functional Moves Towards Defeating Depression

There are various ways of start managing depression that include the need to foster fellowships, getting things done for yourself, or figuring out how to feel improved about yourself overall.

*Continually help yourself that the inclination to remember depression is
Brief and you will deal with it in time.

* Try to converse with another person. I realize it is hard, yet you
should foster force and the initial step is normally the hardest however generally important.

*Put yourself in new circumstances where you will meet individuals. Lock in
in exercises in which you have certified interest.

*Meet with individuals of comparative interest, Join social orders like church gatherings, associations and others.

*Quit paying attention to desolate melodies (for example Without help from anyone else - Celine Dion).

* OPEN yourself to others first. Try not to anticipate that individuals should share their issues with a shut individual

*Try not to pass judgment on new individuals based on past associations with old individuals.

* Attempt to see every individual you meet according to another viewpoint rather than bring critical.

* Cozy kinships for the most part grow bit by bit as individuals figure out how to share their internal sentiments.

*Try not to hurry into personal kinship by sharing excessively or expecting that others will.

*Don't simply look for close connections. Non-romantic or even relaxed mates can be incredibly good.

*Have an even existence. Never disregard great sustenance, practice and adequate rest. One of the primary drivers of sorrow which prompts depression, is the absence of those things.

* Investing energy alone will assist you with looking at yourself all the more intently.

*Don't be a parasite to your companions. Assuming you look for them for sympathy what's more, compassion, they will show up for you. Be that as it may, assuming you over and again drone again and again about your concerns, it turns into a disturbance and your companions will, best case scenario, simply engage you.

*Consider back great recollections and remember your good fortune. Get familiar with another ability.

*Progress in accomplishing something will cause you to feel great about yourself.

*On the off chance that you are having long haul depression, it isn't inappropriate to look for Clinical guidance. It is entirely common to get a solution on the grounds that absence of specific synthetics in the body is additionally the wellspring of wretchedness also, can be dealt with without any problem. Assuming we feel hungry and look for food, having the right medication in appropriate measurements is the correct method for handling wretchedness also, feel less forlorn.

*See a guide and talk in protection.
*Invest energy in Supplication.

# Chapter7:Breaking the Disastrous Cycle

**A fair warning:**

Try not to carry on like a legend since you are desolate.

You wouldn't believe. Self indulgence is an unpretentious type of pride. Pleased individuals magnificence in their accomplishments while individuals who self indulgence magnificence in their sufferings.

It is truly risky to abide too lengthy in dejection since we are made to have associations with each other.

A solid piece of human instinct can't be deleted. Assuming that you grew up living

alone in a wilderness, you will most likely collaborate with creatures or plants and talk to them in your own language.

*The best concern is the point at which somebody abides too lengthy in their depression these couple of things can occur.

*The depression fiend avoid all endeavors to reconnect delivering their individuals around them bunches of agony when their endeavors to help the individual gets dismissed.
*The connections around them gradually disintegrates and when individuals start to overlook the desolate individual, they will feel more legitimate when they at last shout, "Take a gander at them; I was correct up and down that they never really focused on me by any stretch of the imagination!"
*The depression fiend ultimately gets invulnerable to the aggravation and embraces depression as a lifestyle. He is too lethargic to even consider evolving.
His sickness spread to other 'survivors'. This ought to propel you enough to make a move.
**Try not to stand by, do it NOW!**
**Here is an intriguing statement:**
**Depression was the main thing that God's eye named bad.**

# Chapter8:Tracking down Our Motivation in the Wild

Here is a story intended to inspire you. At the point when the residue settles and we have brought in all the cash on the planet, arrived at the level of popularity and gotten the encapsulation of force, what gives us genuine importance throughout everyday life?

Many living things need each other to make due. On the off chance that you have at any point seen a Colorado aspen tree, you might have seen that it doesn't become alone. Aspens are found in groups, or forests. The explanation is that the aspen sends up new shoots from the roots. In a little woods, the trees may really be all associated by their foundations!

Goliath California redwood trees might tower 300 feet up high. Apparently that they would require incredibly profound roots to moor them against solid winds. Yet, we're informed that their foundations are very shallow - - to catch however much surface water as could be expected.

Also, they spread this way and that, interweaving with different redwoods. Locked together along these lines, every one of the trees support each other in wind and tempests. Like the aspen, they never independent. They need each other to make due. Individuals, as well, are associated by an arrangement of roots. We are brought into the world to family and learn right on time to make companions. We are not intended to endure long without others. Also, similar to the redwood, we want to hold each other up. When beat by the now and then awful tempests of life, we want others to help and support us. Have you been going solo? Perhaps now is the right time to let another person help hold you up for some time. Or then again maybe somebody requirements to cling to you.

**All in all life has a significance be careful and have a magnificent life.**

www.ingramcontent.com/pod-product-compliance
Lightning Source LLC
LaVergne TN
LVHW052115160826
845678LV00015B/3573
* 9 7 9 8 3 5 2 5 9 9 0 5 1 *